Self Portrait in a Dark Room

poems by

Matthew Cariello

Finishing Line Press
Georgetown, Kentucky

Self Portrait in a Dark Room

ACKNOWLEDGMENTS

"The Bedroom at Arles" was published in *The Ekphrastic Review,* 11/12/19.
"Hands" was published in the *Journal of New Jersey Poets,* summer 2025.
"The Brown Sack" was published in *Rust & Moth,* Spring 2025.
"The Sun in the Sower," Self Portrait in a Dark Room" and "The Palette" were
published in *The Modern Poetry Review,* Summer 2025.

Poems entirely in quotes, and all quoted sections within poems, are taken from
Van Gogh's letters, as published in *Dear Theo,* edited by Irving Stone. Other
poems freely borrow Van Gogh's language, ideas, and images.

Publisher: Leah Huete de Maines
Editor: Christen Kincaid
Cover Art: Vincent Van Gogh, "The Sower," 1888. Image in the public domain.
Author Photo: Mia Cariello
Cover Design: Elizabeth Maines McCleavy

Order online: www.finishinglinepress.com
            also available on amazon.com

Author inquiries and mail orders:
Finishing Line Press
PO Box 1626
Georgetown, Kentucky 40324
USA

Contents

Life is probably round.

Vincent Van Gogh, *Letters*

The Bedroom at Arles

to see as a child sees
world ordered   one thing
at a time me & not me

two paintings
drawings
chairs

a window opens two ways
one bed two pillows

my pitcher my towel my glass

my door
my floor
my mirror
my hat

three shirts
one more painting
above my bed to
watch my sleep

every thing
its own
color
its own shape
& size

come   home   come   home
home   come   home   come
come   home   come   home

Prayer

fast for one
day & then
before light go
out into the
street & keep
running until no
one can see
you until your
legs fail &
the breath catches
in your throat
understand
this body must
give itself away
in secret there
can be no regret
no longing for
what was never yours

Wheatfield with Cypresses

neither mother
nor father remember

the way the wheat field
spilled from the tree

sinewy & oceanic
the angle of descent

inevitable every
thing in terrible

motion I was 3 this was
my first death every

thing goes away
it said everything

flees overturns changes
places with stars

& asks to be left alone
already the path was taken

already the arc was set
already one tree or two

lights the way already
trying to find my way

through the drowning
grass up toward that tree

Mother & Child

when distant relations
the mother big-boned
long-armed

when the face severely angled
due to the angle
of the pose

when the mouth tightly
shut eyes shut
huge hands

when clasped around
the child's back
who (neither

girl nor boy
armless &
immobilized) stares

at mother's
face not sure
if the embrace

is love or longing
or a third thing
unnamed

Studies of Hands

sun through trees
broken branches of light
in the prism of morning
spokes of the wheel
that comes rolling over the earth

they know the secrets
unfold the folds
hold the roots firm & roll
them in their palms
they are the first sign of life

consider the tender jointed bones
packed in like bees their fragility
solidness curves creases & folds

five starlings on the grass
five rivers that flow two ways
ten waterfalls that rise
all phases of the moon
the vine on the ground
a mother's breasts
the crescent moon lost
an open mouth
a hook
bird beak & tongue
the tree rising into light

Still Life with Coffeepot

every   occupies

        thing

        space

but   holds

        space

        nothing

Leaving Home

"when I stood
on the steps before
Mr. Provily's school
watching the carriage
in which Pa & Ma
were driving home

one could see
the little yellow carriage
far down the road

wet with rain
& spare trees
on either side

running
along the meadows

the grey sky above it
all was mirrored

in the pools"

His Sermon on the Mustard Seed

if you nurture
that which can't

be seen but only

felt like sand
scratching your palm

then you endure

the long patience
of trees

then you suffer

the nest & the bird
then you serve that

which has only one

purpose
to leave

let this lift you up

Imitation of Christ

the miners live
without pictures
without even knowing

what pictures are
they can't read
you speak in plain tones

but quickly for slow
tongues signal deceit
& miners distrust

anyone not caked in black
soot who hasn't slept
among the slag

for three generations
the miner longs
for the earth

the way a sailor wants
the sea & so
you went into the mine

& found that beneath
the earth
many toil for little

other than toil itself
this you imagine is what
Jesus meant

The Long Brown Sack

each of us carries behind
a long brown sack cinched
tight filled with regret
for whatever we can't abide

when the burden becomes
too large to suffer
lay it in the road kick it
in the tenderest part make it
cry in pain

then fasten your tie
about your neck light
your pipe comb your hair
& sit very still for
as long as you can bear

Bible & Candle

that shadow follows
three steps behind
& all night asks questions

when you turn around
to answer it's gone

& so you spend your life
turning from one
ghost to the next

Sunflower

thousand-eyed
along the south
bows humbly
I will go there
lay my body down
& wait years
for the silence
patient I
thousands of small

bloom all summer
wall already
toward the earth
in my nakedness
beside that wall
& find some use
that lives inside
will see how
deaths become one

Yellow Wheat

rather the black cypress
that all things catch on
as they slide
along planes of light

this not the marbled sky
that slumps
not the wheat that
slips & falls

this not
green boulders
bushes & hills
that revolve in
place

rather the black cypress
that leans against the slope
of descent
both in &
out of it

Wheat Sheaves

among the wheat grows weeds
& so gather first
the weeds then gather the wheat
into sheaves & bind them
& stand them in the field
where all can see the weeds
have not taken the harvest

the weeds? burn them

28 Reasons Why

1 your fervor 2 your filth
3 your lack of grace 4 your
inability to stay inside
the lines 5 your selfishness
6 how you hate your father
& 7 abuse your brother 8 how
you love faithfully those
who will never love you back
& 9 how you hate them for
your own faults
10 how unalike we are
11 how you pay whores
to paint them & then 12
want to marry them
13 your crooked floors
& 14 profane colors 15 those false
horizons 16 faceless figures
17 formless trees 18 the lines that
refuse to converge
19 how you ignore me
20 the way you steal the blankets
& 21 soil the pillows
22 your bad breath &
23 rotten teeth 24 cheap
tobacco & 25 revolting
absinthe 26 how you wait so long
to wake up & then 27 so
quickly sleep again
28 how you never shut up

The Sun in 'The Sower'

in the heart of
the field

split with a
sprouted stump

a bright concavity
pulls down the day

a hole in the sky
into which light is drawn

a long way inside
& dragged & hauled

across the earth
color's siphon

shadow's conduit
the sower's arms

circling
in the dark &

the sower striding away

The Child with the Orange

my hair is like
the daffodils green & gold

my blouse is like
the sky my eyes

my skirt is like the sea
what I eat is what I am

what I am is too large
for two small hands

hair sky eyes skirt fruit
take it from me

our last meal pure light
is made without food

Pears

All his still-lives were a form of self portraiture.
Marc Edo Tralbaut

1

here here are these
here they are
these ripening fists into which
light is drawn take them
let them strike your face

2

perched on the edge
of a blue precipice &
prepared to fall
through a prism
while below
the audience waits happily
anticipating disaster

3

curled in the belly
of a wave safe in the roar
of that silence an invitation
to die

4

round & round
the fragile balance
blossom end to stem end
round & round fruit piled high
for no purpose save
the clarity of it

5
talent without discipline
without patience &
ambition isn't talent at all
but a flair a knack
an eye for what's pretty

6
but since
the eye is round
you came to think
more in circles began to
see that to see behind
the object creates the
object even when the line
is strong the space itself
leans & tilts so that
whatever is in it will
roll & the eye will
follow & rest
there

7
the pears are unable to speak
put them in your mouth

8
so much hunger
I could barely hold my brush
long enough to finish
then I gave them away

Self Portrait in a Dark Room

it's lonely being alive
& so I paint another
face for company
who stares back asking
what else will keep me
from my self?
& somehow I'm happy
with this knowledge
of my failure

A Chair

in order to make it
as difficult as possible
turn everything

from square to diagonal
pitch floor tiles
toward the right

brace four posts
with eight rungs three slats
the right front leg

just missing perpendicular
just missing parallel
to the door at the rear

which lends its color
to the yellow chair's border
in the rush seat

a pipe & tobacco
harsh rewards for
exacting labor

Sunset

two parallel rows of bare poplars & the sun between half
blocked by a walker with a heavy load into which light is
thrown this night no other a method to see the invisible &
thus one tree catches fire same as the sun

Shoes

they wait not
breathing all night
without complaint
then carry me
to the streets

yet the stitching
always fails the sole always
wears through   too soon
the heels drop &
split & without
my feet they are nothing

The Man with the Pipe

the head
bisects
the difference
then red
then orange
behind
the wall
just as
something
sees
each eye
sharpened
face clean
white batting
fur hat
green coat
of smoke
form
is a
line
only

The Palette

all things can be drawn
in some kind
of circle the hands &
the face trees clouds
& all things
eventually return where
they were born

sunflowers
lean toward earth
stone walls ceaselessly
crumble & streams
solve the problem of water

the palette already
knows where it's going
& knows where it's been
"ochre (red yellow brown)
cobalt & Prussian blue
Naples yellow sienna
black & white
carmine sepia vermillion
ultramarine gamboge"

remember these too follow
principle eventually
every color every judgment
becomes that for which it is named

The Black Box

for painting in the fields ceaselessly at midday a simple box
big as your head with hinged doors painted inside & out
black for when the light is too strong for when the colors
blend & pale for when your face is scorched & eyes burn
from seeing inside the cypress wheat hills clouds sun stars
starlight on water tiled roofs stone walls rows of blossoms
twisting paths & veering streams then open the doors &
open your eyes & climb inside to rest at first appears the
antipodal world but then even that fades & all that remain
are the wings of one black crow

Self Portrait in Blue

the body bears up
for a certain time
then look back
for a thousand yellows
& see only blue
the coat that covers your shoulders
your lips & eyes & edges of hair
the air around you a mingling of blue
never so clearly was blue
each color your palette could hold

A Response to My Critics

once again I stand
at the sea's edge
bemoaning my fate
at the hands of idiots

I'm finished I say
I commend myself
to the current's mercy

between ocean & shore
I walk a long time
until hunger sends me home

eat
they say
drink

The Portrait of Dr. Gachet

"I have more ideas
in my head than I
could ever carry out
but without it
clouding my mind"

he who sees me
as I see him is the man who watches
my watching & so he bends
to my eye

I repeat

there is more in
his head in my mind
than my hand
could imagine

& so more

of me

I repeat &

"the brush strokes
come like clockwork"

The Church at Auvers

knock & the door will
open ask
& it will be given

but always in twos
fish & snake
bread & stone

two paths
or one   that circles
so that to leave home
means to come home

our last house
is roofed in red tile
the same as we are born in

The Lamp of the Body

The eye is the lamp of the body, so if your eye is sound, your body
will be full of light
                    Matthew 6:22

therefore I say
don't think about
what you eat
what you drink
what you wear
consider the corn
the way it burns
flaxen saffron
consider the grass between the ruts
along the road
back to the wilderness
somewhere past
horizon's edge

consider the crows
how they neither sow
nor reap
& the sky that has no choice
but to blacken each night
& so I ask you

who by worry
would ever add one day
to this life?
what I will do
is nobody's business
I am free to do what I like
with my body
cut myself open
I will spill my light

The Bedroom at Arles

the pain inside feels like sadness
I told Mrs. Hall & she sent me
to the nurse Mrs. Jennings who said
I could lie on the grey vinyl couch
until it passed I was learning
to read that year & learning too
how to avoid the daily labors of noun
& verb grammar sentence syntax
hourly drills of getting it right the
couch faced the wall where hung
on the left an eye chart with
its sad hieroglyphs of failure but
on the right was another room's
secret portrait askew all yellows & reds
& blues two windows two pillows
two chairs the careening floor
& staggering door a counter image
of the school's ordered brick
& parallel lines to lunch I
was thinking sixth grader
because the perspective was close
but not perfect it was almost right
almost a room I could live in back
in class they were perfecting
the period the comma the capital
letter I was turning on the verge
of another sentence slipping
on the vertiginous floor of the room
in the wall where I had never gone
it was telling me a story getting
it right wasn't the point I would lie
there long minutes listening
to my insides turn & surge not
getting any better & not wishing to

This is **Matt Cariello**'s fifth book of poems, following *Colloquy on Mad Tom* (Bordighera Press, 2025), *The Empty Field* (Red Moon Press, 2022), *Talk* (Bordighera Press, 2019), and *A Boat That Can Carry Two* (Bordighera Press, 2011). He's had stories, poems, haiku, and reviews published in *The Journal of New Jersey Poets, Bennington Review, Voices in Italian Americana, Poet Lore, Evening Street Review, Modern Haiku, Indiana Review, The Ekphrastic Review, Modern Poetry Review, Typehouse, Sheila-Na-Gig, The Journal, On the Seawall,* and others. He's currently a senior lecturer in the English department at the Ohio State University in Columbus, Ohio.

www.ingramcontent.com/pod-product-compliance
Lightning Source LLC
Chambersburg PA
CBHW022045080426
42734CB00009B/1249